To Corinne
from Rose
2021

The
Old Man's Poet

BY CHRISTOPHER ENG

DORRANCE
PUBLISHING CO
EST 1920
PITTSBURGH, PENNSYLVANIA 10238

Dorrance Publishing Co
585 Alpha Drive
Suite 103
Pittsburgh, PA 15238
Visit our website at *www.dorrancebookstore.com*

ISBN: 978-1-4809-9337-2
eISBN: 978-1-4809-9301-3

The
Old Man's Poet

ENG'S REFLECTIONS AND UNIQUE INTERPRETATION
OF THE NATURAL WORLD WILL CAPTURE THE MINDS
OF READERS YOUNG AND OLD.

*"We are symbiotic with the world's tree. We give them
the carbon dioxide they give back oxygen"*

TELLING

Just a tale or two, and I will be done just to ramble
On. I will not keep you long, lend an ear for a moment
Or two; I will take you places where only poets reside.
The recesses of inner thought, shadows in our minds,
Come out jumbled, tumbled, and discordant, but after
A while as I sleep, they will come together to keep.

CHILLING

The gray waves, darkened blue white caps there, add
To the hue wind, blown froth around under water.
Riled silt is brown; high above the trees will bend.
Colors have just begun, horizon line softened by the
Haze, the curvature of Earth but carefully shown; the
shores turn white as water hits stone and curls abound.

Big Bend

Pine and juniper mixed with cacti two worlds
Collide in a jumble; red brown cliffs tower high above
Me to humble even the highest climber, painted black
And gold in the evening sun. El Pico dominates its
mountain scene, its shape jolts the senses, and its
Irregular angles evade easy description. Pick out
Tinaja far from the Rio Grande; it can be seen as you
look for a pyramid and a thin line road. There it is, so
Far and fair. Once the Duckbills plodded there, and
The winged ones flew overhead. Once swamps and
tropical trees and plants dominated the desert air,
But nature has no limits when it comes to pace, and
She will continue to change her face. Chisos dominion
Over the land, each a shifting place, but the grace remains.

BACK

Just now, there was a flashback in time to a
Place without a rhyme lost here, don't under
Stand why the words will not come there. In
My head, I know they're there, lined up somewhere,
Jumbled perhaps, but clear never-the-less. When
I reach for one, it comes undone and fades away
Like the last of day, for a poet, this is a disaster akin
To wearing polyester. Some words just refuse to come;
I try to grab them, but they have no substance, seem
Wispy, ghost-like, somehow untrue. Just now, a flash
Back in time, still trying to find that dim, damn rhyme.

CANYON

There is an Aztec face upon the river stone, most
Don't see, but it is there; from over across the river,
A sign, it is their land by birth from the canyon wall
To the desert girth, curving the green river flow along.
Along the silent rhythm goes to a silent song, bathed
Now in the final sun's glow across the endless visage.
Endless brow flows quietly now, and before time, a
Thought, an eternal mind, a deep channel forming the
Boundary, a gap so narrow, cannot tell from here where
It disappears. Some will follow its sudden path, lost mines,
And other treasures lying there in all nature will abide.
Time to her is not the same or ever be our mind to see.

Re-Visit

I was taken by Frost's poem, the woods dark
And deep, miles to go before I sleep. Twisted
Branches, dark and ghost-like, whisper in the
Faint night, light grey shadow wings overhead,
No sound, this scene had me down upon my
Knees. Soft winds whisper a song, these winter
Woods, such a soulful sight, I could not stay.

FALL LEAVES

Flutter, flitter, fanciful, frolic, dropping there to
The bare ground abounding with gifted treasure,
Red, sometimes gold, and partly brown, some still
On branches, dying, their limbs skeletal, summer
Ending shadows though still there, the never-ending
Cycle, oh, just a loving, longing, lingering, lifting time.

WINTER

Cold now just around the corner, hearth aglow with
Warmth. Tonight, outside a blizzard knows when it
Will come; blinding, blowing, spiteful sleet will spatter
The window, suck the heat. Ice will dam at steep roof's
Edge, forming an impenetrable ledge. Snow so deep, the
Door is covered, white winter willfully bringing all its power,
All its beating. The wind will howl and cry and moan, and
The moon will slip in and out of gloom; even the best
Book in hand will not shut out its mighty mix of the
White nightmare. There, my warm bed is not enough to
Hold back the seeping, slowly colding of my fingers and
Toes, or the nipping at my nose. When all is white and
No shape or form exist, will I perish in this wintry abyss?

BENEATH

Just under the waterline, a fragment filament of
Specious time; how long lingering there, no one
Knew, barely visible, a story told and now forgotten,
Lapping at the edges of mind, another life lost to
Mine. No memory of this other form, too long ago for
A memory to remain, breathing, alien to present kind.
Water's depth, while fragile, still seems familiar to me;
Volcanic ash upon the surface, warmer than usual, no
Special purpose. If I were there so long ago, where's
The mental knowing, nodding nestled in a brain cell?
Neurons not as special then, just below the threshold,
Yet yearning touches me somehow. Listen, don't you hear?

SHROUD

Glass-like surface, mist all around, two loons call, want some
Perch; ghostly trees seem to stand on air. Are they really there?
Skillet washed pan astir, rocks and pebbles clean them bare,
So quiet, no sound, no surf, a soulless lack of mirth. Now, just
Now, the mist started moving across the lake very slowly, as
If to take all the time to go. Sun peeks through now, not hard,
To look at barely seen, not warming, yet clouds now define a
Coming break, motor sounds a burble. There, man casts his rod;
I can see now raptor bird in a dive lake has finally come alive.

PARTING

Don't know when I started missing you, came on slowly, like
Running glue. All the bad things were gone, only the shiny
Memories abound, mind's way of softening the ebb and flow
Of life's crabbing, scolding, pouting, only now in soft refrain,
As if there was never any lingering, wholly possible pain.

FIRE

Licking flames and blacking soot, hungry wants,
More wood thrown on in orange flames, held
Back the night, just a moment to gobble quick.
Blackened logs did not burn, await next days;
Fire nearby, hear the crackle, pop, and hiss tear
As smoke invades; eyes water, hurt rising high
With woods beyond the fire ring, holds its kind
Lest any flame escape to sear my coat or singe
My brow. Will not, as London's saga wrote, fire to
Warm the coldest night push back the fears
Harbored in sentient light in the darkened woods?
Move more by flickered light, yet the silence
Beyond the pit holds me close, will go to early
Morn when coals die out, and rabbits feed on
The chunks left over the warm glow, gone now.

WIND

Blessed, blasting, boastful beast, a west to eastward
Sound swirling round held to ground, backing off,
Then from east, silence not its usual plan. Raging,
Restless, ruthless range brought again the soulless
Bane up the down slinging sand, wanton, whipping
Devil's hand, moaning spiral band, came back hard,
Down thru ages, turning its earthen fan just once
More to hear it blow, just once more to feel its
Pace cross prairie grass stretched green and tall.

ROCKET DREAM

Liftoff minus ten, or so blue wisps and
White, yellow, red flames do flow; black
Grey smoke trail back, crowd shouting
Over rumble sod, shaking ground. Round
Faces, bright eyes, look up; heads nod,
Necks strain upward, children cry. Two
White tracks cover sky as they arc away,
Brilliant orange glow in array. What will
He say, challenged by fragile life today?

JOY

My heart beats a rhythm burst like hymn,
Want to run at lake's rim, break through
Trees from dawn till dusk, a song's blend,
My head rings rapture, send timeless end.

MOVEMENT

Travel to the timeless land, browns, gold
Growing. There, waves ripple across the
Tops, bends banded grain to every hand.

CRAZY

SONG, LIGHT, FLICKER, DANCE
MOVE, STEP, TOUCH, AND SLIDE.
SING, TALK, WHIRL, AND PRANCE,
THEN SWAY, DAZZLE, DIP TO YOU.

BLACK FIRE

Flow crater to black river, molten fire,
Liquid rock, white sand, desert shimmer,
Large, dark cone with shadows side-by-
Side, mixing with the casting clouds so
Random dot this land in mind. The ebb
And flow of time ridges, caves, and birds
Explore, home to ravens, hawks, and more;
Lizards hide in cracks of oldest volcanic
Lava flow, sweet breath of spring created
After fire and steam and pyroclastic flow.

HALLS OF TIME

Echoes from past tombs stretch misty time lost,
Every word upon a loom, aged, crackled, creaking moss
Was a mind before known time. Voices timbered, soft
Whisper lilting, long ago what treasures more than
Barter, kind, tinted colors, gold sublime, blind me to
The real kind, yet no knowledge or reasons rhyme.
Fraught with delicate threads, no wells of tears or
Wells of joy bring a heart to catch the metaphor of
What's left behind; somewhere lies the answer dear.

BACK COUNTRY

Split rock, broken shards, sand bleached shore, and
Remnant snow; sun glint, ice broke, hard dappled
Shadows wave in cold fingers cool, tried to feel,
Slippery line broke, rippled pool, quick, dark speckled
Fish. Hands sore, still no fool, heels dug in aching bone;
Need this meal, sinew, strong rumble, belly down below.
Wind wept and wind did flow, sun low, spring dark chill;
Soon, long dark leaf lost in tree spikes, the umber sky.
It broke surface in my pan, fire hot and a ready hand.

SLIPPING

Wind blast cross valley draw drift below snow;
Too cold grabs breath before its raw backs
Down, drop to knees, frozen crawl, under aged
Pine to grave, hollowed icy snow-bound drift. Wind
Blasts ice crystal trail, already into ground; needled
Covered inner line still green, hazy vision of summer's
Door tempts me to sleep, eyes glazed over in a dream.
Return to life, barely there, cling by thread though
Thread is bare, yet something feeble burns want to
Wake blood; sluggish movement slow, also want to go.
Soft snowflakes drift outside, burial mound only guide,
Want lovely, lingering, longing grace will to live might
Give away spring of life rivulet; now, take back death's
Scepter's blade, robed evil today, will not have his way.

Boom

Long before the pyro flow, long before the magma rose,
Before the beasts roamed this land, before the shallow
Inland sea, yet not even a continent did see. Why do we
Fear to bother or to prevail over trifle matters? You may
Blink, and it is gone, long before a careful coolness's grace
Layed down, and to this day upon its ancient strew, how
can such a thing be written, such a thing be thought?
Just now, the moment hangs in the air, yellow, mottled
Soil now laid bare, just a whisper, just a silent prayer.

BACKWATER

Small shack, weathered board deep in woods dark,
And green waft of smoke chimney toward heavy
Sky, dusk's ruddy gleam, Gas lamp lit on hewn table
Stood dappled light on cabin wall; haze in poles,
Rafters should, children sleep in lofts so tall, pipe on,
Curled lip, adrift, thoughts wander, not out loud,
Clearing frosted ground brought this place from
The crowd, nothing here of modern ilk, all that's
Here to give life; its song to live, to love, to stay home
Free. This is where he wants to be nestled, cozy, warm.

BEND

Curved round the oak tree, green dappled, burble
Brook, shadows swim in murky breath movement,
There then to look back before ancient time. Was it
Where the present stood, or other liquid flaming
Glow uplifted, swam, and current slowed? Yet now
This leafy glade green and ripple down below runs
To water salty sea before time began a single sun.

BEND

Curved round the oak tree,
Green dappled, burble brook,
Shadows swim in murky bree
Movement there, then to look.

Back before ancient time ago,
Was it there, or other rock
Heaved about midst flame glow
Uplift split, strewn to mock?

Yet now leafy, glade, green be
Ripple below quiet, slow run,
Running to a water, salty sea,
Back before time began a single sun.

BACKGROUND

Glacier water linger near rippling, burbling, do
You hear rocks that talk and sound so queer,
Crows that bark, green tall pines that sing as buzzards,
Wolves that howl as they must do? Stones impede
Your course, gurgle some of, what's the source dragon
Flies go as they please, tracks along a road attest to
Others, here perhaps to drink, lapping at the brink.
Like us, perhaps nature's at her best when only looking,
Observing her in her nest, sometimes the surface flattens
Like the backs of loons unruffled, no breeze, young pines
Adorn the far lake shore old, beyond time, as before.

PAINTED HILLS

Quiet start, white blue-tinged sky, grey to white
Expanse tinged hue, shrubs indistinct gone to
Purple view, no wind, no sound, quiet, still darking
Mountains, some light though fading, slow parts
Of light green cactus, show yellow tinge near
Horizon line feeling intertwined, touching some
Thing unknown; grey clouds go black, now silver
Moon shines behind, not quite risen, not quite time,
Loss of color draining from every bush and flower,
So dark now, wait till morning light; no first star, yet
Tonight, some fear lingers from primal time, want to
Hunker down in warm light, all blanket round and
Tucked into my delight drifting, drifting away to day.

STILL

So still all night, so quiet, no light; a whisper heard yards
Away, who's to say? Who opposite of the day's riot, the
Only noise comes from the star's next days; rocky road
Tosses my gut to and fro like a leaf in a gusty swirl. Dust
In ringlets rises high in the magical, misty light of the
Stillborn reef; fossils lie older than known seawater gone.

BLOCK

Ho hum, humdrum, no fun. Oh well, got to tell a story
About a mystery so deep on insight alone. Not to
Worry, writers, cramp taking toll words, won't come;
Black pitch sits there, hath no fury like words dammed
Up. A story bold lurks somewhere there to wrench
Your heart as you look for gold. Ho hum rain now
Patters, the quick wind, then the thunder makes a
Call—oh well, if I could fat the pen, make a magic stew;
Writers woe welcomes and withers me to have words
So near that I could touch just out of reach. In some
Rut, a line may fall on paper yet, and perhaps the
Ghostly pen would rhyme still; the will comes late at
Night when sleep draws down, wakes to jot, wrack
My brain for nuggets naught to come at first light.

DOWN AND OUT

Cash gone, bad rags, keen tribute sounds silent.
A ragged king still not to singe the soul, lifeless
Longing round bend too far to fly away, yet near.
Still voice deep and dark hassles me in the park,
Bites like hell, sling the hash, cash gone now, sad
Mutters the voice, just a waif wringing hands,
Wanting wings; some will lift, some will pass,
Some, giving up, will hate, hurt, and hit the wall.

Its

Green hills shadows still stark relief, stable reef
Rocks yellow-gold, red-brown, and purple shade
Against the almost frozen hill trek on foot, where

Mist

Wispy, milky transparency, light grey to white, wrung
From sodden clouds, pervasive seeming non-ending;
In its endless drift, almost a dream world edges,
Unknown, not sure of the present clime, prefer more
Visual world to rhyme—my rhymes just now large
Drops of water, fall, making wet spots on my pages.
There is a poem here, I am sure for the ages; there
Is rhythm to the rains vertical but vacillating, fall
Later, no unbroken sound as a creased forehead,
Frowns more time than solitude as a protective,
Translucent blanket covers me in this northern
Wood. I neither seek shelter or scurry away there;
Is something here I need, something that I should
Pay attention to? Just not sure what; as my pen waits
Some thought of mine, let me see what time to go.

GIVE AND TAKE

Bird sing, repeat song; singular sound wolf answers the
Moon. Not related, you say, but part of the pattern of
Darkening dusk; there is a pleasure here in listening
To the sounds. Now, an owl who hoots rustles, yet now
On silent wings, hear the wind catch its tune, sometimes
Mournful and sometimes hoarse as it passes through
The pines. Something scurried hurried, just then, a patter
On the fallen leaves scratching, scraping branches against
My tent, sound on gravel, a camper bent to find a spot
Before the night. The soft lapping of water as it lisps
Against to rocks, the ticking of my watch marking the
Always passing time, do not break the mood, do not
Break the spell as I drift in and out of sleep, time will tell.

PINE LAKE

Abandoned bobbers floating there, ripples playing with the lure.
Where are the fishermen? Beware, you are in Davy's lair; wind
Blown lattice, all shades, dancing across the water, they fade.
Next to edge is wooded glade; the rocks on shore seem to sway.
The deck upon which I sit is weathered, worn with aged knit,
A bit nostalgic, I will admit as my mind wanders to child's trip,
Paint peeling, but shadow, sun dappled mix; dragon flies wing
And hover, flying insects take care, for they are quick as silver.
Small minnows dart beneath the dock, protected here before
They grow, and many a fish and fisherman will want to know
Their where-a-bouts and when to move their rod and reel.

CALLING

Heard just now a silent shout, not sure from where it came
About, yet it was there, this I know sounded helpless from
Far below, distant, feeble mind aglow with its meaning, I don't
Know, want to measure its undertow whence did it come.

CONSPIRACY

Paranoia prattle, picking brain, James, dead or alive
Again. Gunfire blazes along the main down in Kansas;
Drinking gin Ford, were you the one? No DNA match
Is done. What important, unknown clue leads to the
Death of another man? Billy, just south of the Rio Grand.
Guns firing at the pursuing band, fancy hat not usually
Found on a New Mexican horse is lathered mouth to
Foam; weather's grim, storm clouds above, nothing here
To care or love. Sun-baked and saddle sore, rain would
Help, that's for sure; horse now lame, nowhere to hide,
But trusty Colt at his side; not this time, Billy, its yet to
Come by another man, Pat Garrett's quick lightning gun.

BACKBONE

Sled dog to the front, snow swirling round others
Tethered behind wheel dogs' closet to the runners.
Blended wolf puppies sometimes raised for their
Courage and tenacity; tendency to lead through
Blinding blizzard. On the trail, they cannot see
Whirls of crystals all around. Where's the sky? Where's
The ground? Musher lost in silken shroud but still
Controls the sled's direction. Camp fire and food a
Must; warmth will mitigate, callous, cold trail saga
Still unfold until, at last, the end is near eyes to tear.

GONE

Power block, hemi free, crazy plum color be
Faster to the topping rise; tires screech, rubber
Cries, wind is left far behind landscaped warped
To the rear Mach has nothing on. This car whistles,
Creaks down to the tar, dusty swirls at desert's door,
Sandy whirls round the star, throaty rumble exhaust
Does roar, flashes, then its chrome decor mirage or
Just passing, fancy, lost again on roads forever gone.
Just a speck, then surely surfaces then nevermore.

Essence

FREE BE RISE, SIZE, REAR GEAR, THROTTLE FAR,
DOORS BLOWN OFF, PAINT IN SUN'S GLARE,
ROAD, GOAD, ROAR, SOAR, LINES ON BLACK TAR.

OLD BLUE

You sit there in the sun just baking and pull me back
To long ago, mind wanders back to Idaho, waiting,
To a time when youth aglow. How many miles have
We gone? Your small rear engine all revved up, faded
Now, but you still bedazzled my dizzy heart, chugging
Along, hup-de-hup. I am so proud of you and remember
When you were new how much of me is intertwined
In the memory's so kind. Remember when your fabrics
Were new, and your blaupunket radio? Your skin did
Fairly glow, run on, my little beetle, go! Your spirit sends
Me along another longer, winding road.

STREETCAR

Yellow now, it rounds the bend, clickety-clack on that
Track, down ninth street, drug store bound, it ends
On turn-a-round. Blue uniformed men with gold tie-tacks
At each end turn car in half circle to be city bound
Again. As a kid, I made swords from two-headed nails laid
On the track; now, riders board to the city of lakes, past
The Moline plant, through wood and dale, an elevated
Track across the marsh. Deep in my thoughts, they carry
The mail, the sisters, brothers, and dads; dedicated were
these engineers as the sparks flew from overhead
Electric lines. These cars dominated the rails in a time
Gone by, I will ride and dream today of yesterday say.

BROWN MOUSE

From deep woods the creature came; he
Would not leave his name. Every wilder
Creature known, his antics mimic ghostly
Moan in a paper bag did rustle to find a
Nibble here and there; when nothing there,
Got his fiddle, played a tune in my head alone,
Would play for a bite to eat, yet he could
Not find a treat. Did an owl chase him in silent
Wings upon the wind, now quite at home, want
To nestle in my clothes, seemed a bit too
Testy, yet what would draw him from here away?
There was something silly I could not say.

WARM SPOT

Found a place to warm my gloves, shoes, pants,
And socks on a cold winter night, just above the
Stove. Love the small cabinet there that will house
My gear, tired of freezing in the dawn, so took a
Look at options near, then it hit like a bag of rocks,
Grabbing my brain, whirling within, discovered that
Place toasty warm, a place to put all my things. Warm
Socks on cold, bare feet, toasty shoes adorn, lowers
A warm tee shirt, jacket, long pants, just the way
They should feel now. I could hike the Chisos, the
Chimney Rock, the yellow butte feeling warm and
Ready, safe yet cozy; this heated spot, Robert Service's
Magee never thought of that? He would not be quick
To jump his stove if he knew what I know now this
Simple method to feel this well in freezing drizzle
Or coldest woods; no other way to feel so good.

STORM

Woke to rocking, tossing, ruckus. Rain slashed
Green night air, soul shaken heart to mouth,
Nature in a whipping frenzy, a terrible night,
Blinded fright, to slash the light washed misty
Middle night. Rain driven sideways, I may be
Dreaming, yet so real, home shaking, uneven keel.
Could death come on storm's swift heel, sworn
This morn to feelings' sense, witness all its power
Score as it blows as an ethereal, endless roar.

MYSTICAL MOUNTAINS

Cloud veiled, shrouded unknown days last…
Never ending nights to dawns break clouds' lift,
Shone gleaming surreal peaks. Do my eyes glimpse
Enough light to make out Chisos peak, clothed in
White, now real, now slight, unending brown
Dappled by sunlight? Conjure up this breathless show
Not compared to any more delight there, reeling
Reason through all those halls to see nature's ability
Written on the land. Just stop and stare, sun popped out
again from clouds above to shine its feeble light upon
The dome now altered, different, angelic. Shone below
Stood a tiny gnome struck by small and mammal kind
When senses pounded by earth's great feats eternity,
Not blind to all that's wrong, but brings such bliss once
More, my gaze on top on hill, rumpled stack of rocks
And snow, wonders more as we will dream above.

RAPTURE

Crystal clear, yellow gold spike the sky, deep blue
Capture sun sure and bold flow from scape below.
Ernest faces lit back there sank to depths as I knew
Face of orange and red and shadow fringe flare,
Follows flow from edge of diamond ring, then glares
To green half sun, half shimmer, dark seems to
Hedge white apparition. Azure sky green bristles pine
Below thin atoms of air on high, only toss of will.

WIND CAVE

Sunk here beneath the hill's prairie grass rife
On top and rock deposited down below,
Ponderosa grace, steep ravines, such is nature's
Delight. Shadow mist and filtered light have
Combined in subtle setting homage to the
Hand is wrought in the passages down below
To have mocked short-sighted plans of man;
These halls of grandeur dot the land.

Gum Drops

Gum drops, tasty bits in the woods, candy,
Pleasure, succulent by mouth and sugar;
Dew cannot give them up in tent beneath the
Darkened sky, spice drops, yum and double fun.

TIMELESS

With no horizon there, warped by hole black and
Dim curved back on the selfless sphere, infinite
Whim sucking where also in ancient mists so thin
Was blackness stretched to endless matter, energy,
Squared distance has no meaning; it's just a jaded
Junker jump from a funky far-flung future time
Contraction when relative thus light and back again.

POLAR

Silent drifts of virgin snow low, crags of blue and
Green winds beyond measure blow nature's beauty;
Rings of true water lap at still floes edge erosion.
At micro pulse will planet girth allow a wobble, cause
Ebb to ice winds, blow white in crystal mist can bear.

SPIRIT

Power has its rightful place, may move the
Cauldron fire, not known whether light or dark
Whispers softly might be restless here or
Restless there, ceaseless, endless tune, backdoor
Moving near the gate is movement there or not.

COLDEST MAY

Will it ever get warm? Cold blast of northern air
Should be tee shirt weather gear; already three
Layers on my torso, saw my breath early morn, so
Forlorn under blankets lie, feet like cubes of ice,
Lumps nose tip as cold as ice, last of May, you are
Kidding—can't get nature to do my bidding; should
Be flowers and warm rain, all I got is joint pain. I
Will move to balmy pole, lay there on a beach,
Have ice tea with music, lay in snow enjoy dip in sea.

MOONSTRUCK

Fog hanging over glacial lake so misty, hard to see.
Possible loch ness does lurk, years strip away oldest
Fossil, shadows drift out and in, ghostly trees might
Be Ents or other beings… what else may lay beneath
The water, unseen yet there? Formless rocks, cannot
See the other side, hidden in mist and curve; lake is
Endless life song, flapping wings sings the eagle.
Timeless life, timeless death theme interwoven so
Fog so thick now cannot see, longing lake, whiteout,
Then no sky or ground eternal would this scene
Forsake endless misty, working, waterless sound.

SUNBLAST

Mercy, sun, you're so hot, melted asphalt, boiling pot,
Mist long burned away, mighty atom fission lost;
Flare a million miles high, flashing sunspots as I sigh.
Fumerols are cool next to sky, finish the job, and heat,
Solar wind swept north, neon sail on blackened pond,
Seek a radio wave to sound solace in a long-time bond,
Implode slowly after swell roads to majestic magic dwell.
In some billion plus years, well inside a white dwarf will
Tell the final tale of a midden star which gave its all long
Ago. Time will stretch, tiny, life-giving ball of cinder, we are.

SPIRIT WORLD

At the deep brown water saw misty rock
Lie foggy across water teems with unseen
Lives there or by the wisps of dreamless
Waves slapping sound against the stone.
All the time this time same to stay in this
Land where spirits talk collective conscious
Of all before now gone, yet waters and the
Pine hold their secrets and their lore. Is it
Real or some other cosmic rhyme? Do the
Pine and water whisper? Don't dismiss out
Of hat, for that's what keeps our spirit caged.
I will open unmapped distant parts and chat,

BOTTLE

Wind washed shoreless fall message reflects,
Water backdrop of timeless wall restless ebb,
In falter drifted soulless depth below whirled,
Sand trackless drift clouded filtered sunless,
Glow dreamlike sifted visions gift current run,
Turtle flow slight rip under slide ran to shore,
Sand below scoured bottle etched in tide young,
Then old is all the distance but where this land,
Lost long ago never found whatever sky and,
Reddened sand pink then gold then yellow to,
Burst from water float atop ran the curved,
Wave mellow dropped to the waiting hand.

FLIP

Start at the end zone, head to the region, so
If this is a mind bent tone, bother not with foe.
Warped space, black hole go embryo, floating
In liquid, not knowing the beginning or the end.
Awaken to the historic id, curve back and gain
Time or change space to fast, slow, before or
After climb reverberate, vibrate at last... lost.

BACKBONE

Born of poverty, salt of earth worked to bone,
Beyond belief, hand with dirt round the thumbs,
Crops spring full, no relief, died there; though one
Seed did bloom, the others all went to virgin death,
Fruit of the earth, long of the planet will always till.

PINE AND ROCK

Jacked up against hills of green, rock and juniper hug
The sky, bursting pine cones are seen; white rock
Sentinels at night, at daybreak, blue sky scudding
Clouds to run the rampant horizon range, yet rain
Forecast today may bring some life some think to
Nature's tune. These bluffs set in rolling plains
Rippled earth from whose hand soft rock, shale, or
Fire came with tan brush and finer flower, whose
Brush has painted such tones and left it right here.

SUNDOWN TOWN

Next to the Carlsbad gap, a town called white's at
Sundown hills bathed in soft grey hue tone dotted
With cacti and animal stone, small old west town
With storefront façade stucco off white in soft glow.
One can imagine cowboys long ago, rigs in and out
All night long up to see that cavern far below grocery
store with old man at the counter. His white hair bobs
And weaves as he sweeps; the floor keeps things bright.
You can buy treats and other delights parked there;
Tonight, to wait the gas in the morning, many times to
The cave now just want to go down to the next wood
And glade full of cave wonders and bat sonar sounders,
Full tank of gas slept the night tire, sounds daylight bright.

GUT

Running out days to go, supplies dwindle, spirits low;
Ration beans and weenies, so how long will they last?
Don't know… nothing left now, just the water. We'll live
On that. Does it matter people have starved while in
Laughter, hallucinating a feast, a glass of beer hereafter?
Still under the seat, found some pancake mix, another
Stash I had forgotten; some eggs, too, need to kick this
Eating habit; three pieces of candy, I will eat them now.
Enjoy what is left; we'll make it then life, is short anyway,
Anyhow, bow to desire, gobble them up. There are wild
Raspberries and blueberries out my window there.
There may be hope to make the month, this seems
So much, but five days yet to go, I don't know, must not
Tarry, looked at my gauge gas tank's empty — oh Mary.

BILLION

Billion years, one or two, makes no difference, we
Have only a few of these to make our notch. Rock
And sediment, magma flow, too many eons to unfold;
What importance do we entail, small and frail, to the
Massive expanse of time? Nature is the dollar; we are the
Dime, cracked and grazed by heat, greater to imagine,
Yet our minds are capable of slaying that dragon. Up
against a universe so immense no one can deduce its
Exact dimensions, yet we try to list boundary tensions
In mind, wrap it in a package, neat and sublime; billions
Of years, our lives a drop of water in the salty sea of time.

RATTLESNAKE CANYON

Twenty-one drops of rain on my windshield, that's
All the desert southwest could cough up. Drought
For sure; cold as ice, the air at night… did its best.
Canyon leads away beyond my sight, drops down deep,
Shadows, hole snakes sleeping somewhere out of
Sight, small mammals need not fear to roam. Small
Dirt road leading into morning light does not detract
From rugged height, sets me dreaming about what might
Have been long ago in this ancient scheming reef. In
Still, another guise so hard to tell, built of tiny creatures,
Stacked one on another when under water they lived;
Out their lives, under my feet, under the dust layer, I walk
Upon my step, only a small twinkle in the eye of God.

Not Sure

Didn't ask for it, yet I'm here; not sure, but destiny
Or not life has sprung in this spot. What to do with
This awareness, not sure—it presents a nebulous
Flurry of outcomes; some probable, some not. When
Not aware, unconscious, so to speak, no problem.
Not sure the purpose of the vastness of existence,
Nor the long history; what's important, what's not.
My mind sometimes slips out of the normal passage
Of events and goes somewhere not completely in my
Control, usually results in creative bent, yet rent with
Uncertainty. Not sure why the body and mind slowly
Fade in a kaleidoscope of unfinished business; when it
Comes back, I am happy, I think. Not sure of the global
Nature of our infinity, scary it would seem… not sure.

WRONG

Bird song gone wrong, butter pats, flip cakes, hell to
Pay if I burn the beans. Got no money and little brain;
Downstream, paddle lost, eerie sound of the river roar
Splintered round, a host of noises under the superior
Shore. Agates rocks of all ages battered by waves so
Cold have no sense of sages who live on the other
Shore. Hare bounds down to nibble leaf, pebble skips
Along the beach, another source, a silent tiny tear.

WHAT

Green eggs and ham are Seuss's own language to
Encourage or interrupt the creative hand, and
Though danger lies in mental sigh, absence of malice
Is not denied. Most really don't care; virgin forests and
Seas sublime existed long before bi-pedal time if only
To communicate in the rough, Dr. Seuss, I hope you're
Not too circumspect, but fair to say, it is a better bet to
Play our hand to write a line between the line, and yet.

ANOTHER CASCADE

Cascade river, down you run; your potholes rage.
You have nothing but fun with water spraying
And flume hissing to the lake in jagged drops.
Longfellow said it best: to some, there's beauty in
Nature's rush, hum the rhythm to all she's done.
Drink deep the wine before the sun glistens golden;
On the run one moment, here, an eternal pun lingers.
Squeeze and kiss, toast the one who matters most.

MAKE IT SO

Adventure in the darkness of space will be a spiral galaxy
Or nebula glow; thrusters on vibrations flow, set in the
Course, set speed Mach One, and make it so, helm, lets go.

FARMER

Don't know what to say man… hard to put in
Words what you did for me, the trust you
Understood. Each step I take reminds me of you,
The bard who said life's fleeting moment is but
A walk across a stage, a mote in time for a life; to
Me, after care and strife and silence cut, you were
There for me when it seemed that nothing
Mattered, not even dream all shattered in a
Moment's silly rut to lay it all down in a gambled
Bet, for you would say it matters not. Team your
Horses to your plow, cut the farrow, pound the draw,
Buck up the day, begin again to live a life almost
Forgotten, then grab the reins say hee to haw. Drag
Your plow, it's your field today; earth to black loam,
I will not nag or tarry on the way the field is done.

SUPERIOR

Light grey misty lake pines, stark black against the
Backdrop, no iron ore boat today. Have they gone away?
Split rock light just a glimmer, small pulse of light
Against the break of day seems like a long way away.
Where do the sky and lake end, and the earth's curvature
Begin? Eternal rift between heaven and lake or land's
End, mist, fog, then light rain paint a surreal picture again.
The lake now slightly darker as the clouds bend to
Touch the water; people ghostly as they walk the shore,
Not sure they are really there. Voices, though eerie in this
Light, come drifting across my way. Will the sun ever
return to burnish the beauty of this land? Don't know,
Not important. Somehow as I am right now, of course,
Its bleak and somber; were they ever there? So alone at
This moment, suddenly shadow, then thunder, I don't
Know what ancient puzzle or puzzler caused this show.

TORRENT

Cascade river, down you run; potboil rage endless,
Way first, big lake, and then evaporation to cloud
And back again. As rain, you have the fun; I can only
Watch nothing but water spray and sun adding to
The sum of water in the deep abide. Longfellow
Knew your beauty as he sang in poet's song; he was
In touch with nature's hum. There is a rhythm to all
Said and done; drink deep the wine that will come
Cause air is free if unspoiled be, and the water's
Lair unfettered with anything but floating leaves.

DIRGE

Snap-crackle-pop; often heard that sound as slurping
Down. I did a wonderous song, tasty to lip and tongue.

GRASS

Cool, breezy prairie ocean, wheat-like flowing brown
And green wave in pensive seething motion; song
Sing lark meadow, scene distance, knowing seeds sowing.
Life giving heart sounds, insects abound, black bird
Curving wing; paths through blue blazed sky gifts from
Nature on her swings, coyotes howl later at the moon
Given then to roam and curl up as night creeps along.
It's cold, cannot go to a grassland so bold where bison
Roam; thunder hoofs in distance quake, then munching,
Chewing, lay their snout, strange, haunting dream about.

Schizophrenia

Not to seem to obtuse, but really what do you
Mean? I heard one thing; you said another; too
Fragile to understand, your drift carried away
Upon a wordy wave, here but not here as the
Echo of your sound touches the edges of my
Mind. I would like to engage you, but am unable
To put the sentences together—oh, another voice
Intervened; I will be gone for a terrible while.

SUNFIGHT

Battle of the titanic clouds add sun, all day relentless
Without thoughts of crowds; first clouds to rain, then
Gone again as the sun chased the hazy blue mist, utter
Devoid within the clime till none the haze. Part sun, part
Cloud, just another ordinary ocular, oceanic day.

BIRD

Bird sing repeat song coo; wolf answers wolf to moon.
There is a testament to woo all; nature's there to swoon,
feel the wind catch its time, wild and free we will never
Be. It's their fate, and ours, too, some other God may say
Change this or that; it may be misty rain or different
Human shape. It's now however and never will be enough
To stop the two-step tangential trail of timeless time.

BIG BEND

Saw deer today when morning light cast against the rock
First hit the peaks in the basin. Soulful watchman of the
Night, such a place is sometime Chisos, sometimes alien,
Sometimes so soft I could wrap within; it would cuddle
And caress as I went to dreamless sleep. How long has it
Been this beautiful? What volcanic power created this
scene from golden peaks? A fiery force drove up the land
And pyroclastic plastic flow formed diagonals of layered
Cliffs to bring this awesome spirit heap; it's hard to leave
This primal place, mother's womb, the human race, the first
To be woven on nature's loom. Weave what you will,
nature dear, I will be here to drink the heady wine of
Of sweetest taste of your pervading grace, just a wink.

MULE EARS

Windy caste to bright blue sky punctured by dark
Daggers nigh stark against a lighter golden brown;
Red rocks mark the footpath's way, century plant-
Like chamber doors line the trail spiked green azure.
Wonder fills the mighty soul of a land, so barren, yet
Drawn to come again, yet again to feel its power, see
Also the mighty towers old fighters flew through to
Practice. Then, small birds flit from plant to plant; agave
Grey-green fills the scene before its time to call its
Name. It changes and leaves us stunned to endless
Change in endless time. Buried beneath thicket and,
Yes, coral lies a dark pool; to hear its longing trickle,
Just this water left of shallow sea to hear the earth
Itself talking whispers known only to the guiding light,
Mysteries so long uncovered, not in the mind; some
Other place, endless rhythms, endless rhymes.

Re-Visited

Trek on foot, ancient buffalo path, stumble, catch
The mountain thrill; pure joy bursting busting forth,
Feeling what they must have felt, beginning time.
Perched in cliff, gray-brown hawk, no need to reason;
No need to talk, inward spiral closed on me diverts
And lofts, swirling up beating wings, now just a speck.

Music

He has always been in mind same age. Are we from
The iron? Are his roots where the words come from? I
Do not know Viking heritage, that's for sure; rebel
Sound now honed right here, fought the battle in
Outrageous bellow roots with other trackless
Fellows seared my brain, grabbed my heart humble.

Duh

Peace in the valley for assholes abound; no need
To resist, for they will take you to town. Oh, they
May talk in sweet terms and honeyed tones,
But put down your guard, and they will jack you
Around. Some think they are nice but can't you
See? Treat them right, and all will be light.
Assholes abound, as you will see, peace in the
Valley but really watch out for the weeds.

CLOUDS

Clouds move, scudder through faster than trains do.
White and gray, soft but persistent to make pictures
There if you wish. Friends gone by or passed this way,
These clouds tell us to perceive the day when all is
Spirit or passed away. When all that's written fades
Away, it seems sometimes that you may touch their
Undersides, so close they seem, I am lost sometimes
In an unpardoned uniform yet breathtaking dream.

CLOUDS AGAIN

I know that I can touch the clouds; sometimes, it seems
They're right on the horizon line, yet if I were an angel,
Time ailerons are sublime and touch the universes.
Behind reflection, it seems cures my ills today; just wait
Though, those clouds will pass away. I will be back
Another day when the chaff in straw goes away.

RUTS

Long ago on prairies' grassy bluff felt the weight of
Wagon wheels, the Platte River crossing, rough narrow
Gap up the hill. Iron clad wooden spools sought the
Earth traction gained, turning damp dusky sod upside
Down, sun-drenched, heated ground sent wafts of heat
Skyward, bound to blue bleached arc and hazy crown.
Squeaky hubs and crickets chirp as riders found no
Cushioned seat, pounded bones and muscles ache; sun
Bleached canvas, flapping, whipping side to side, pulling
Oxen, sweat drenched glistened hide, maybe twenty so
Today, but what cost sunrise to sunset toll buried there
Along trail's way? Oats and grass and sometimes hay,
Blackened pots, fires, tray, some walked all the way from
Missouri border to Pacific bay, the blue emerald ocean.
The ones who made it said it best, God bless those at rest.

SOLAR

Fiery red blooming orange furnace fire, magnetic fuse
Gravitations, immense force galaxy wings, universe muse,
Million years like a day beyond mind's ability to pray.
Where is the logic to say what power holds us today?
Inner atoms in a silent chain combine to yellow main;
Controlled explosions feign something hard to say in
Verse, only us, or is there more to look or to explore
Inside that seething powered core, solar sail ion, or more?
Red giant swallows whole planets as sun abdicates soul,
Now warped beyond all control.

Chaos

One moment's too long song, life fritter fruitless way;
Dark matter invades all of space, saucy soulless say
Physics governs all sporadic curving wells of time.

NATURE'S WISDOM

The mountain much older than I, both have
Snowy head, still I feel not bolder than nature's
Grand poser peaking up behind her hills. Purple
Front, granite gray, light tan prairie front still
Fades to distance; say what has more to do with
Life than all wisdom and lore of our stinging
Wit. She has us beat; she has us for the range and
Beauty, so vast expanse dwarves the poor works
Of man in all past, no infinite wonder or quest.

Passings

Fragile life, wisp of smoke, your essence hard
To touch. Fleeting memory gives up hope
Sitting there across from me; watch reflection on the
Wall, funny laugh knew right off that you could see
How tall the tales that I would spout; ask the question
Oft will be in a spirit resting, how far, how close will
Be right here, over there, round the corner, or above,
Beyond the edge, can I care? Drifting slow away,
Ghostly memory soften flow not remember all the
Days when together we played, leaving loving light
Dim, now not always felt, knowing that you're there

Fog

On cat's paws as Sandberg said, the trees ill
Defined in this wintry clime filled the dale,
Filled the lake in definition or scene to take.
Am I asleep or am I awake? This dream-like
Vision has no supervision or insight, just as
I take delight in the surreal fog as it turns to
Night; around the corner is a small dim light.

BIRCH

White against the misty lake, a splash of red as
The rain would create a water color painting
As real as this sight, the horizon lost behind the tree,
leaves are gone, white skeleton with back spots
Are left bare, twigs defined in the misty air there.

REVERENCE

Rocks of every tint and kind, red, pink, yellow, green,
Purple, orange, strata hard upon soft upon hard bind
Each other in nature's sculpture, primordial glue a
A working sign sat still to watch the javelina drink,
Cautious as they broach the pool. Close I am, and
They know but see no threat and no attention pay.
Ravens chase a covey of quail, flutter fly into the bush,
Sandy butte, dark relief serene and quiet. I gain strength
Beneath, yet voices speak, and dishes clatter. Water runs,
And people matter, does not disturb my resting mind,
Miles away from that darking pool, yet I am there again.

POISED

Just at the edge of conscious mind, not lost not yet, but
Near a place where worlds come together, melt into one,
Spirit and organic cause passage from one to the other.

TROLL

Beneath the earth, a fearsome man beset by
Fairy tale and myth Scandia lore and maybe
More, hiding in closets or imaginary realm will
Come out and either be helpful or sore. No one
Knows how this got started, but fertile minds may
Have begot it. Children see them as potential
Friends, yet are afraid of their possible ends; I
Personally would like to meet one, just to see if
It would interact with me or somewhat hostile be.
When the mists of mind and time unravel here,
Will I be near or far away? Here tomorrow, gone today.

RHYTHM

Flicker fly birds on high near the heavens' clouds
Soar and sweep as they dive deep to catch that
Shadowy, slippery fish, then back to the blue edge
At horizon's limit, now just a speck, a dot, a mote
At the edge of Earth in the eye of the jaded man.

STASIS

Just let all stop; for a moment, hold still, hold life
Dear, not slow motion, but a stillness bounded by
Quiet; no aging, no passage of time, no expanding
Universe, no rotation, no movement, ah, sublime.

TALKING TREES

Was it real, the wind, or the rustling of the leaves?
I thought I heard something just then. Were they
Gesturing to each other, the language of the Ents?
Or was the rush in my ears just my inner voice?
Mottled sky caught glimpses of the sun, but it did
Not stop the chatter or, for that matter, the conversation,
Continued. When I am not here, are they still talking?

ICE

Blue white, then green glow shining in the light,
Beauty in a cold place, peaceful in the night still;
The full moon caused a stirring in my heart as
Yet another peaceful sight left me melancholy.

EVENING RUN

Rapid river run rampant, wet stones, bleached bones;
Sparkling spring, sunlight glancing back, golden eye
Shaded, silky, springtime tree blown boldly in the breeze.
Budding, burnished new life, leaf open to nature's call;
Yawning, yellow surface, glow shadow, slinking at back.
Worn, etched shoreline rock, logs lurking in the muck;
Empties, endless at lake tide flashing, frothing as alive,
Milling, munching fish abide, lost and linger in dark side.

DEATH

Godless, mourning life's other side to no avail, as it will
Come in like a landslide. Don't try to hide; its guide is a
Spector with caustic robe, inevitable in his long guise.

ALONE

At the wall of many tears, a crypt and tomb align,
A message of love and grief. Were you ever there,
Or is the myth just that? No more I have heard your
Voice and felt your presence, indistinct and unclear;
Many have cried and gnashed their teeth, pounded
Fist, and cursed their luck. Is it all fable told in story,
Yet real somehow at the edges of my mind sometime?

GONE

Death so quick and spirit to fly against a headwind
Rest, then as the night settles in soulful darkness then.

CPSIA information can be obtained
at www.ICGtesting.com
Printed in the USA
JSHW042013100321
12129JS00005BA/14